Pieces of Me

A Collaboration

by
Terence Perrault

Pieces of Me

Pieces of Me

I dedicate this book to my three kids, Terence, LaTeidra and LaDeidra Perrault.

My kids are my inspiration, my strength, my purpose in life, and have been from the day they were born. I want to be more than just a father. So, no matter how successful this book is, I will have shown my kids that you have to take chances in life to reach your dreams—they are not just given.

I want my kids to tell the world "My dad didn't have much, but what he did have, he gave to us... and for a moment in time, he was an author. He accomplished one of his dreams; his signature became an autograph."

Note to my kids: I will love you guys until my last breath.

Table of Contents

Pieces of Me

Pieces of me…

Spiritual Journey

Pieces of Me

Mysterious yet nondescript as a letter standing alone,
He stands.

Tall and upright and confident in the man he is and has
become.

Strong in opinion, bright as light, tough as the life he
has lived and overcome.

Loving and compassionate, yet distant and aloof.
Though unconcerned about the things that doesn't hold
his interest.

Easy to laugh and will curse out in anger with the same
breath,
He stands

Slyly he smiles like the memories of his youth are ever
present,

Remembering his conquests and physicality and
prowess,

Holding on to good times, living in better times,
looking forward to the best of times,

Pieces of Me

Still striving for the unconquered dream,
He stands.

Aware of the attraction that calls women to him yet
unimpressed by their longing,

Having had his fair share of physical intimacy he longs
for something more,

Looking for the one that will bring balance and awaken
his sense of belonging to that *one*.

In the meantime, he waits without looking and looks
without seeing.

Consumed by his need to find, to define all that God
has for him,
He stands.

Intelligent, powerful and knowing,
He stands.

A father, son, brother and friend,
He stands.

Complex and simple—an enigma,
He stands.

Determined to bring out the best in those he loves,
He stands.

Pieces of Me

As good with his hands to labor as he is with a pen to
write,
He stands.

Unwilling to accept anything less than truth,
He stands.

Open and eager to confess all that he is and not,
He stands.

Pieces of Me

In Development

We breathe without thought.
We dream without cause.
We feel without intention.

We grasp to understand those things that hurt and
anger us...disturbing our
spirit and inhibiting our rest.

We breathe without thought.
We dream without cause.
We feel without intention.

We grasp to understand those things that hurt and
anger us...disturbing our
spirit and inhibiting our rest.

We reach for things that are out of reach...like a child
reaching for the cookie jar on the highest shelf.

We find joy, happiness and wonder from the
unlikeliest of circumstances...like an unexpected phone
call

Pieces of Me

Or a dog excitedly running with his reward from the
hunt.

We look for acceptance
And requited admiration from unexpected
acquaintances....like an old friend or a new stranger.
We get lost in wonder of what is and what could be yet
We find peace when we realize that everything we are,
hope for and hope to be....are
Simply in development.

.

Worthy

You seek to be greater than God.
He cast you out of the garden so you can see how
you will struggle without Him.
Some of you will lie, steal, cheat, kill and
suffer without Him.
Though some of you will do well, but you will still feel pain
and hardship as though you were in a living hell.
Without God, there is no such thing as a greater world,
life or person;
there are no pearls.
So go out into the world and see for yourself that greatness
is only achieved through Him.
When God thinks you are worthy of standing beside Him in
the garden,
only then, will He call upon you to join Him once again.
Your loved ones should not be worried that you're gone nor
should they speak with stones; it was His decision.
He knew it was time to bring you home.

Are you worthy?

I Promised

Vulnerable, susceptible, not sure—a feeling of insecurity

I promised myself

Encounter, bump into, come across—a feeling of meeting.

I promised myself

Adolescent, undeveloped, fledging—a feeling of being young.

I promised myself

Postponement, anticipation, time lost—a feeling of waiting.

I promised myself

Age, maturity, senior—a feeling of being archaic.

Pieces of Me

I promised myself

Picturesque, astounding, extraordinary, nice, lovable,
stimulating, young,
Free, intriguing—a feeling I have to know.

Damn!!

I broke my promise.

Promise: a declaration that
one will do or refrain from
doing something specified

Clouds.....

Floating, hovering and oddly approaching

Circling and pressing against all it can find

Opening, closing and allowing droplets of moisture to escape

The air that emits is warm and wet, like fog

Yet it leaves you feeling oddly cool,
As if a breeze has encompassed you.

You look for them and think they have floated away.

Yet they return,
The next one even more beautiful than the last

Floating, hovering and oddly approaching,

Soft, billowy and caressing,

You can't escape them.

You turn your head and they find you again,

Floating, hovering and oddly approaching.

As the clouds get near, you shiver

Pieces of Me

You want them to find you.

You want to see and feel their softness again,

Yet you don't want to get lost in them.

So again, you turn your head and cover your eyes,

Yet they are floating, hovering and oddly approaching

And once again, you are lost in the
Clouds.

Just Breathe

Thoughts have come rushing in and my mind won't let me focus

On things or situations or people or places that used to be important.

I long to inhale and exhale deeply to confirm that I am in control.

I remind myself that it's important to take in the air that sustains life

Yet the pain in my chest won't let my diaphragm expand and I can't remember how to breathe.

Trying so hard to clear the clutter in my mind and to recall where this fog began,

My recollection of when this began has been muddled and I can't find the beginning.

Maybe escaping into the night will allow me to process all that is known and unknown.

I feel like an amnesiac with memories rushing in and my subconscious is fighting against things that are too painful to recall.

Pieces of Me

As I venture into the stillness the cool breeze is
liberating;

The briskness rejuvenates my soul;

The dampness against my skin feels like purifying
waters that will wash away all that is hurtful or
frightening.

I attempt to rebel against my body and forcibly attempt
to take in that which is required for my sustenance.

We are taught that this is an involuntary motion;

The brain knows to make our heart beat and our lungs
expand without being told,

Yet I am suffocating and fighting for every breath.

Maybe if I pick up my pace the need for oxygen will
be so great that my body will once again remember to
accomplish this most simple task.

I am smothering in my own thoughts, lost in place and
time.

Maybe the depletion of my breath is causing me to
hallucinate,

Pieces of Me

Like an astronaut in outer space I drift and dream of
things I've never seen

Yet I am able to breathe there.

The salt from my tears has alerted me that I am only
dreaming and must find a way to correct this
malfunction.

I awaken from my dreamy state panting and thankful
that my brain has not abandoned me;

The oxygen and nitrogen are again in harmony and I
can breathe yet I am still fighting for every breath.

Once again I feel the pain in my chest

My heart and lungs are in discord

Seemingly angry with one another and the cacophony
of the beats and the breaths is disturbing.

I realize that I can't fight this process.

I must deal with the unconscionable and on occasion
remind myself to just breathe.

Pieces of Me

God Gave Me an Angel

Pieces of Me

Her wings were bruised and broken.
She tried to travel a road that was unspoken.
She had everything in life she wanted…
By using her first token.

Pieces of Me

God gave me an angel

Pieces of Me

She never thought her wings would be bruised, broken,
or tired;
She took great care, giving them all the attention that
they required.
Now she sits at night going over it all
As her heart beats in fear.
Looking up asking *"What did I do wrong?"*
As her eyes fills with tears.

Pieces of Me

God gave me an Angel

Pieces of Me

If this was a love story then I would have no worries.
This is about a young lady who has lost her courage,
Trying to hold on to something that has put her
feelings into storage,
Having lost her wings and finding it hard to see clearly
on some things,
Forgetting God has paid the cost that she is pure,
beautiful and needed.
You are your own boss.
Let no child, woman or man put you on a battlefield
that you don't understand.
Jesus gave his life one day for all our sins.

Pieces of Me

God gave me an angel

Pieces of Me

Just don't sit there defeated, stand up and breathe—
Your body needs it.
Sometimes life needs changes;
So open your eyes, your mind and your heart.
God never wanted you to stop here and dwell,
He just wanted to give your life a brand new start.

Pieces of Me

God gave me an angel

Pieces of Me

Yes…God gave me an angel

Pieces of Me

Connections

Restlessness

Loving you
Gives me meaning

Restlessness...

Loving you
Gives me reason

Restlessness...

Loving you
Gives me joy

Restlessness...

Loving you
Gives me strength

Restlessness...

Loving you
Gives me purpose

Restlessness...

Loving you
Gives me happiness

Restlessness

Not knowing…
Gives me restless days and nights,
Not asking, for fear it may push you away.
So I stay in a kind of limbo engulfed in a warm gooey
feeling and relentless panic.

Pieces of Me

The First Time

Looking out of myself into a world I can't believe,
seeing a figure that is so intriguing,

Not made with hands—untouched by flaws, seemingly
unapproachable as she stands,

 But not standing still.

Her branches are moving rapidly as though a swift
wind is trying to send her in different directions.

As the night levels off it brings a calm relief to her
limbs,

Fagged from the vigorous motion of the wind

She reaches deep down into the earth's core for
nutrition, as two leaves slip off to the bottom of the
floor,

 Although relieved from the situation,

A sudden voluntary movement startles her as it
approaches the area.

It casts a shadow over the base of her young body like
a rain cloud.

Pieces of Me

Soft thundering words, followed by a gentle rain
pour to wash down the earth's core,

As the rain stops, it leaves behind seven rain drops.

Looking out of myself into a world I can't believe.

The enemy

Efforts to draw near...compromised
Communication...stalled
Signals...blocked
Directional devices...scrambled

Can't find my way
Fog dense
Clouds low
Sky dark

Where are you?

Vision blurred
Senses dulled
Bones stiffened

It continues to block my path
Miles and miles of emptiness
Roads and highways apart
Land and oceans that separate

Do you see me?

Pieces of Me

I'm reaching out

Clawing and climbing
Trying to emerge

I can't fight alone
Throw me a lifeline
Send a life raft
Call for life support

Don't you hear me?
I'm fighting the enemy
Yet you won't assist
I'm succumbing

Are you afraid?
We can close the distance
Narrow the path
Overcome the enemy

If only you would reach for me

Stolen

No matter how hard you search you can't find it.

Knowing that it was where you left it,

Neatly tucked away in a secret place,

Safe and protected by all of the locks and alarms that barricaded it,

Yet it's not there.

So again you search

Over and over again you question yourself,

You know you didn't move it and it should be where you left it.

So again you search.

It was so important that you know you didn't give it away.

Could someone have been lurking around and discovered your hiding place?

Pieces of Me

Would someone have taken your prized possession without any remorse?

Yet if they did how did they open the locks?

So again, you question yourself.

Could you have allowed someone access without thinking?

Did you subconsciously give away the keys and give them the code?

Was there some unknowing desire to have your gift removed from its seal after being hidden away for so long?

If that were true wouldn't they tell you they had it and rejoice in its ownership?

Maybe you should put up signs and post an ad proclaiming your lost possession and offer a reward.

In reality you know that once it's returned it will be damaged and the value will not be the same.

You can't even file a claim because it wasn't insured,

Pieces of Me

Therefore you must accept your loss.

That very thing that you were trying to protect is gone
and you can't get it back.

After the grief and sadness you will recover and
attempt to rebuild and redefine your missing treasure.

Although it will never beat the same.

Pieces of Me

Broken Promise

I was married for a very long time and I thought
everything was great, but it turned out to be only in my
mind.

You see, my wife, my Queen had found herself
another king, although I noticed things had changed,
you don't believe it until that day you wake up and
your whole life have been rearranged

What used to be, *Baby, let's go;*
Turned into *Baby, I'm not going.*

What used to be, *Baby, make love to me;*
Turned into *Baby, not tonight.*

What used to be, *Baby, I have your back;*
Turned into *Baby, I think you can handle this fight.*

What used to be, *Baby, we are running late;*
Turned into *Baby, I'll meet you there.*

What used to be, *Baby, let's go to the movies;*
Turned into *Baby, you and the kids go.*

What used to be, *Baby, I can't stand my boss;*
Turned into *Baby, I have to work late.*

Pieces of Me

I got so tired of the "what used to be;" it was tearing
me apart.
I dropped to my knees and asked God to give me an
answer to my question,
You are my Father I have no one else to turn to with
my burning heart;

I seek you to show me the way, for I do not know what
King's bed my Queen's head will lay.

God give me an answer; I need to know if this is where
I belong or do I need to move on.

God please give me an answer; I promise I will do as
you say.

Two days later God gave me a thought and I carried it
out; now all I have to do is wait for my Queen to be
caught.

Seven days later God gave me my answer.
It was clear as day.
Pack my bags and move away,

But I stayed…

Only to see my Queen's head go back to another
King's bed.

Nothing

There is something in your voice that makes me warm like a summer day.

Something in your laugh that makes me want to hold you close,

Something in your smile that makes me want to hasten to your side,

Something in your swagger that makes me want to undress your soul,

Something in your attitude that tells me danger is near,

Something in your heart that tells me to find the key that unlocks the past,

Something in your spirit that tells me there is a bright light shining,

Something in your eyes that tells me there is something hiding,

Trying to discover something...

Ultimately leaves me with nothing.

Love Is

The love I feel is so much greater then u and I, for the
love I feel can't be
explained by man or woman, because if the love I
know could be explained we
would dare not to love anyone because of the burning
sensation of pain it leaves
deep down in your soul, because in the end love is pain
through the lost of that
someone, now I can tell you the basics of the love I
know, the love i know is
trust, laughter, sharing, the love I know is giving even
knowing that u may not
receive, love is sexual, love is fear love is pain, love is
unexpected, love is
protecting without wanting protection, love is a
challenge and love is worth the
right type of pain, love is not at first sight, love is
going through a dark
tunnel until you reach the light with that someone,
scared because of what you
can't see, you fear staying in the tunnel becomes
painful to your body your mind
and your soul because you see no end to the darkness,
not knowing because you
are too scared, not realizing all you have to do is turn
around and walk out the
way you came in and start over.
Love is fear, love is pain

Conjecture

Wondering what could have been…

Pondering how it would have felt…

Questioning if it would have lasted…

If not, would it have been worth it…

Asking will the longing stop…

Will the fire extinguish?

If it does, will I want it to?

Will the vivid pictures abruptly fade into memories?

Will the ability to feel her hands and her lips dissipate?

Will the funny conversation stop interrupting your thoughts and cause a smile?

Will your heart stop racing at the thought of her?

Will you allow another a chance?

If you do will you stop comparing them?

Pieces of Me

These have been identified as unsolvable equations with no resolution.

Simply conjecture and the one who can successfully compute the answers...wins my heart.

The Truth

Though his mouth said, who-knows-what,
The placement and assurance of his hand said "This is
just a sample."
Though I had no idea who he was,
My body said, "Girl you need to know him."
Who is this guy who is bold enough to tell me I need to
smile?
How would he know?
Though…
You know I smiled, right?
He spoke to me with his confidence.
He spoke to me with his intoxicating aroma.
He spoke to me with his honesty.
*No one would fabricate such brutal self-
imperfections.*
Again,
Who is this guy who has me wondering who he is?
I listened for the answer…
He spoke to me through words he didn't say.
He spoke to me by letting me speak to him
Through unspoken words customarily solicited at the
initial meeting.
Intriguing indeed…
He spoke to me with his rhythmic lexis.

Pieces of Me

So enchanting, I again wondered, "Who is this man
who knows how to move me?"
Though I didn't ask,
The fun would be in the waiting…
I would wait for him to show me.

He showed me with his lips.
> **M'mm *give me a moment…***
>> *My mind has a singular thought and my*
>> *diaphragm automatically*
>> *forces out a long cleansing breath.*
>> *And then there is a…sigh.*

He showed me with his lips.
> *Yes indeed, it bears repeating.*

I waited...
He showed me with more rhythmic words.
I waited…
He showed me with simplicity.
What is simpler than the truth?
In their simplicity, his words held up a reflection—
Clear and haunting looks of myself.
I can see *me*.
Naked, vulnerable, willing.
How does he do it?
There is no subterfuge, because the truth has none.

Pieces of Me

But his honesty shields himself and allows me to see
the true me.
Who is this man?
I wonder if I will ever know.
Who am I?
Afraid to be consumed by
Wanting, longing,
A need to be touched, wanted, needed…loved.
Afraid to be totally addicted and consumed by him.
Who is this man?
His palm permanently scorched into my back
His voice permanently etched in my memory
The feel of his lips on mine, his touch, his grasp, his
tongue,
His eyes, his wit, his boldness, his uniqueness—
Forever linked to my heart and other places.
Fear is the catalyst that we use to question the
simplicity of truth.
The truth is…
He is the man who wants me to smile.

Pieces of Me

Ghost in My Soul

Pieces of Me

There is a ghost in the air, lingering, hovering around,
binding me, holding me,
who has captured my soul.

But he is not real, he is just a ghost.

Pieces of Me

He emerged from a place that I hide within my heart,
from a time and place so very long ago.

He knew me then and better now; he has the best
insight into my soul.

But he is not real, he is just a ghost.

Pieces of Me

He pushes me passed my insecurities, he challenges me passed my limits and he holds me accountable to my fears; he knows me better than I.

When I awake I feel him near, when I lie I smell him close.

But he is not real, he is just a ghost.

Pieces of Me

I love him so, that I still taste his kiss, I feel his touch,
and I crave his embrace.

My daily thought of a life under his protection, near his
care is just a princess fairytale because it's not real.

There is a ghost in the air, lingering, hovering,
binding me, holding me,
who has captured my soul

But he is not real, he is just a ghost.

Pieces of Me

He Waits

It began as a *what if?*
It returned as a fleeting maybe;
This captivating one who has aroused his nights and
enthralled his days.
Not unreachable just out of reach.

And so he waits.

He waits, not with patience but with conviction,
Convinced that this very basic allure is worth
exploration.

And so he waits.

What keeps him fascinated is the mysterious
familiarity.
This captivating one, whom he knew, is not the woman
he has begun to know

And so he waits.

Waiting for the opportunity to understand that for
which he waits—
Attempting to rationalize the incomprehensible.

And so he waits.

Pieces of Me

Briefly he considers that his waiting is purely wanton;
A fleeting desire to scrutinize the most carnal behavior
of this captivating one,
Yet he knows this very basic allure is more than
lustful.

And so he waits.

And in the midst of the tranquility of his own
peacefulness—the wait was over.
The fantasy and the dream collided into a menagerie of
bliss.
The joy was in the *what if* that was recompensed with a
fleeting maybe.

So now he smiles as he waits.

Knowing that the prize has been obtained.
What he was waiting for is already here....not
unreachable just out of reach.

That First Night

As I swayed my hips and glided my feet to a six count beat, he was posted up at the bar peering out over the dance floor at me. I was blissfully ignorant to him studying me and in a matter of just a few songs he had learned to decipher my body language.

He recognized the intonation of my steps, decoded the flirtations of my movements, and he understood the dialect of my expressions.
Although he was a stranger to me, he could read my blueprint better than I could even draft it.

Several songs, line dances, and martinis later, I now find myself posted up in a convenient red leathery booth that outlined the dance floor.
Despite being bombarded with countless propositions to dance and talk, I shamelessly kick off my shoes, lean back, and stuff as much of this random tub of Tony Chachere's flavored popcorn into my mouth.

The alcohol I'd gulped hadn't turned any toads into princes, but it had managed to persuade me that this Orville Redenbacher was a five star gourmet meal.

With one handful of popcorn in my palm, and another handful stuck in between my teeth my silent onlooker appeared from nowhere.

Pieces of Me

It was the stranger, the mystery man, this creature who didn't fit any known stereotypes.

As I looked up at him with my poofy hair, rumpled clothes, and half-eaten lipstick, this broad-stanced gentleman towered over me with a confident smirk.

Instant shock suddenly takes over my face. The mere fact that he approached me in my couch-potato state is so sobering that it makes me question his logic for stepping to me.

At this very moment, I could only notice that he was different. I had yet to notice his observant, anchoring light brown eyes and strong, skillful ambidextrous hands.

I had yet to feel his soft, affectionate kisses and heart-stopping grasp around my waist. I had yet to admire his rugged, solid physique or be comforted by his dominant protective nature.

The mystery man begins to speak and out pours a masculine, melodious voice that made my spine bend in unspeakable ways. I had never heard a voice that was so deep and soothing before. I mean the man could read a bed time story and put wild boars and grizzly bears into a peaceful sleep.
Then, with a mischievous grin, he continuous to introduce himself.

Pieces of Me

He spoke with such clear and concise language that it made me reevaluate his noticeable open-faced gold that enhanced his seasoned gangster nature.

As I am still in a state of shock and disbelief, he handles the moment with such etiquette.

Out of every man here tonight, he was the only one that had any discretion about casually connecting at the wrong place and time. He was able to see all the flies buzzing around his quarter horse.

This man had a certain unparalleled individuality that struck home.

Unable to put my finger on it, I accepted it without really understanding it.

Our encounter with one another struck up enough curiosity to put his cell number in my clutch. His number managed to make it into the special zipper compartment where a lady keeps her emergency credit card and overpriced MAC lipstick.

Usually a man's number or egotistical business card would make it as far as the gas station trash can by the unleaded gasoline and windshield cleaning brush thingy.

Pieces of Me

And then he was gone.

Just as mysteriously as he appeared, this stranger
disappears into the dark corners of the room to
continue peering upon me without my consent. Not
over thinking our brief encounter, I continue on with
business as usual. I hadn't the slightest clue of what I
had REALLY stumbled upon.

If I had known what was in front of me I would have
ruined it with my young girl nervousness. I would have
never gotten the chance to experience his late night
phone conversations and his cute day time romantic
gestures.

I wouldn't get to hear his adorable chuckle or his
sleepy voice when he tries to stay awake at
three o'clock in the morning. I never would have gotten
to lay my head on his shoulder at Applebee's or see
him kill herds of mosquitoes outside of Waffle House
to stand and talk to me.

I'd never sneak away from work just to steal a
kiss outside of Popeye's or relive every word of Joss
Stone's "Tell Me What We're Gonna Do Now."

And what makes it all so crazy is that neither of us
ever saw it coming.

Pieces of Me

Sensual

Syncopation

The drum begins with a 1-2 rhythm,

Setting the expectation for what is to come—

Hard, pounding licks that rumble and vibrate.

Next comes the sweet melodies of the keyboard—

Up and down the scales with an intensely sharp sound
that makes you take notice.

Just when you have found your ability to keep time, a
new sound emerges.

It's the deep vibration of a bass guitar.

The sound is so rich that your body trembles and your
ears vibrate.

The sound is intoxicating like dark liquor and smooth
like fine wine.

You find yourself swaying and leaning to and fro as if
you must keep time.

You are being serenaded and hypnotized

As if a pied piper is playing this music only for you;

Pieces of Me

Then the horns wake you as if the hypnotist has
snapped his fingers,

And again you are entranced.

Your pupils enlarge as if to encompass this entire
scene.

Your hearing ability is sensitized and you feel as if
every drumbeat is being
bounced off your membranes;

Your senses are enhanced and you tingle as something
brushes against your skin;

You are caught between pleasure and pain but you
have been muted and words will
not come.
So you continue to sway and lean and take in this
concert.

You feel every pounding drum beat, the tickling of the
piano keys,
The caressing of the bass strings and the kiss-like
blowing of the horn.

You have been privileged to participate in this
symphony
And when the music stops, you cry.

A Good Song

As our eyes met across the room
I had a seductive thought.
I wanted to make music with the instruments of her
body.

As I reached out my hand caressing her face as though
I was playing a violin,
Touching her body gracefully as if playing a piano.
Then I stopped…
No, not because I missed a key—
It was the sweet sound of the melody that uttered from
between her lips.

I looked deep inside of her as I pulled her face to mine,
Touching her lips as if I was about to play a song from
a flute,
Holding her face in the palm of my hand then
Dropping down to my knees—
Stroking…*EVERY*… string of her guitar
With my tongue.

Pieces of Me

I hear drum beats,
Buts it's only the pounding of her heart.
As I place my tongue, my lips, my mouth
On the reed of her saxophone…

Mmmm…

What a good song that is.

Aroma

The scent of him resonates through me like the smell
of mama cooking Sunday
Dinner.

The feeling of comfort and peace that comes from
knowing that things are as they
should be

Causes a warmth inside of me that erupts into a cold
sweat.

It's on my shirt and on my skin and continues to follow
me.

I turn to see if he's present because it has appeared out
of absent air.

The scent of him is sweet yet rustic, like aged
molasses—

It's masculine yet gentle like a strong hand;

It's overpowering like a drug and if I'm not careful it
will cause hallucinations.

The scent of him lingers and floats in the air.

Pieces of Me

It envelopes all that it touches and invades me like
smoke from a burning wood pile.

It causes me to inhale deeply and when I attempt to
breathe again I choke
because my lungs are overpowered.

It can't be escaped or denied and must be
acknowledged.

The scent of him is intoxicating and makes me want to
escape to faraway lands;

It causes dreams of destinations abroad and white
sands and clear beaches;

It causes dizziness and panic simultaneously.

The scent of him makes me fantasize of lazy days of
lovemaking and long nights of passion.

It can't be replicated and it only belongs on him.

It is his signature—just as distinctive as his fingerprint.

It is impressive, yet subtle and it is the aroma of only
him.

Chocolate Erection

Walking up from behind,

Pulling your hair slowly from the back of your neck,

Caressing your body with soft moist kisses,

Chill bumps appear…All over your back

Running my hands firmly down your arms

I feel a change in my body…

It's a quiet storm.

With every lightening strike I can feel your body

pulsating…

As you're holding your legs tight,

I put my hands around your waist laying you down on

a playground

With the chocolate erection that you're about to taste

Oohhh….

Pushing your head down to the bed, looking into your

eyes so I can see what you want

As our bodies reach a vigorous boiling point.

Pieces of Me

Reaching out to your face, pulling it closer to mine,

Giving you an unbreakable kiss

That is filled with so much passion…

Putting your breast into the palm of my hand

As I suck…

Lick…

On your nipples.

Feeling the heat from your body

And mine

I get weaker,

But stronger at the same time.

I run my tongue down your…

Ssssss….

ooooohhhh…

Do you feel it?

It's so wet.

I'm licking you up… and down… until

I hit that spot…

You know the one.

Yeah… just like that.

Pieces of Me

I feel your body wanting more.

I come up placing my erection in the warmest spot of
your body.

M'mmmmmm....M'mm

Ahhh...SHIT

Sssss

You feel so good.

M'mm...

I don't want to stop.

My Pieces

Who am I?

Who am I to be arrogant
When they are so humble?
Who am I to be afraid
When they are so courageous?
Who am I to be a quitter
When they persevere?
Who am I to complain
When they endure?

Who *am* I?

I am nothing without the three pieces who makes me whole.

Who am I?

I'm mom and dad,
I'm friend and confidant,
I'm protector and shield,
I'm love and safety,

I am the pieces that make *us* whole.

Who am I?

I am everything to them.

Pieces of Me

Acknowledgements

Special thanks to my collaboration team:

Ms. Natasha Simmons—for being a true friend and adviser and also for pushing me throughout this process—we do make a good team. Natasha is also an author.

Ms. Alena Savoie—a young lady with a bright future who once told me, "Terence, never think you have accomplished enough in life until life is over."

Ms. Jeanette Rodgers—a lifelong friend who has inspired me with her story, which made me want a story of my own.

Ms. Kelly Baldwin—a dear friend of mine who has always told me I should publish my poetry.

Pieces of Me

Dear Reader,

I hope you enjoyed reading my collaboration of poems. It is titled *Pieces of Me*, but my pieces are made up of all the things that touch my life. Many of which, I'm sure, can serve as a reflection of the lives of those who read these poems.

Thank you for taking this journey with me.

Sincerely,
Terence F. Perrault

www.ingramcontent.com/pod-product-compliance
Lightning Source LLC
Chambersburg PA
CBHW071827020426
42331CB00007B/1639